SCHIRMER'S LIBRARY
OF MUSICAL CLASSICS

LUDWIG VAN BEETHOVEN

Symphonies

Arranged for the Piano

by

OTTO SINGER

IN TWO BOOKS

➤ Book I (Numbers 1-5) — Library Vol. 1562

Book II (Numbers 6-9) — Library Vol. 1563

G. SCHIRMER, Inc.

DISTRIBUTED BY

HAL•LEONARD®
CORPORATION

7777 W. BLUEMOUND RD. P.O. BOX 13819 MILWAUKEE, WI 53213

Contents

*The dates in parenthesis give the year of first performance

36517

SYMPHONY No. 1

Adagio molto.

L. van Beethoven, Op. 21.

Allegro con brio.

4

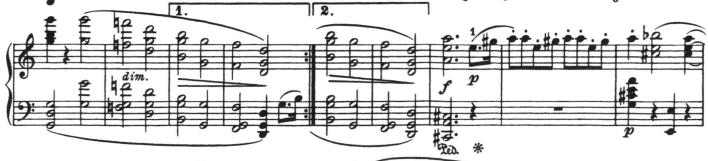

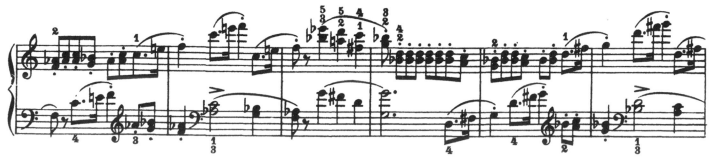

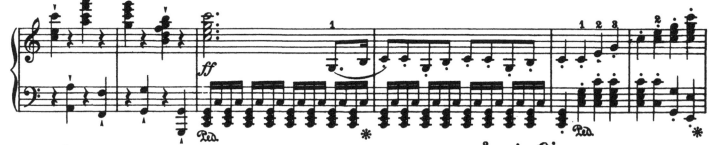

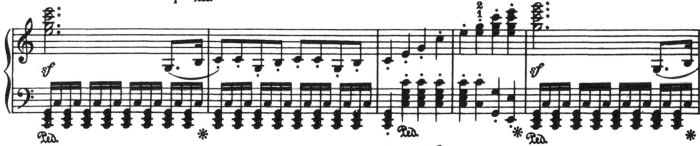

Andante cantabile con moto.

Menuetto.
Allegro molto e vivace.

Trio.

Men. da Capo.

Finale.
Adagio.

Allegro molto e vivace.

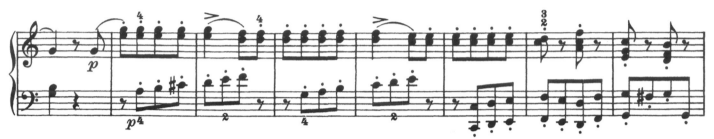

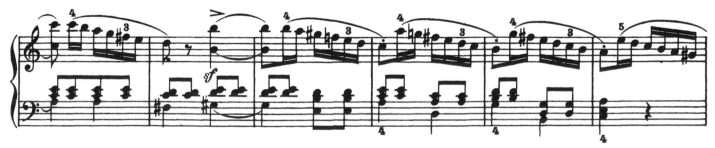

SYMPHONY No. 2

Adagio molto.

Op. 36.

Allegro con brio.

36517

36517

Larghetto.

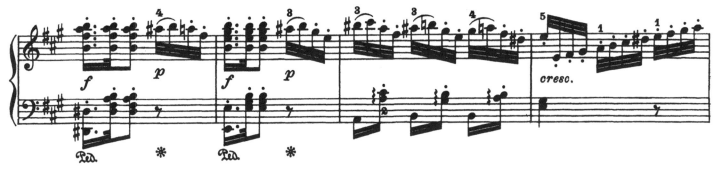

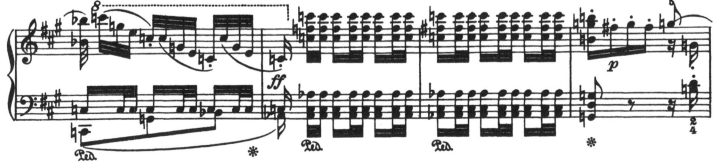

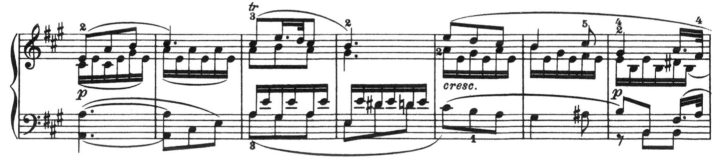

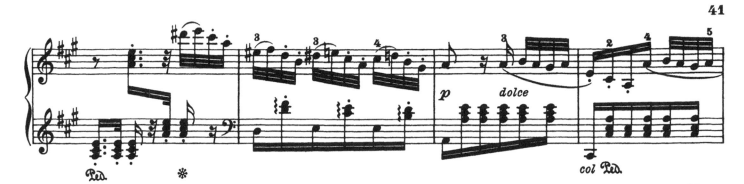

Scherzo.
Allegro.

Trio.

Scherzo da Capo.

Finale.
Allegro molto.

SYMPHONY No. 3

"Eroica"

Allegro con brio.

Op. 55.

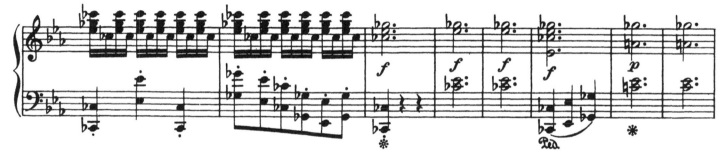

Marcia funebre.
Adagio assai.

Maggiore.

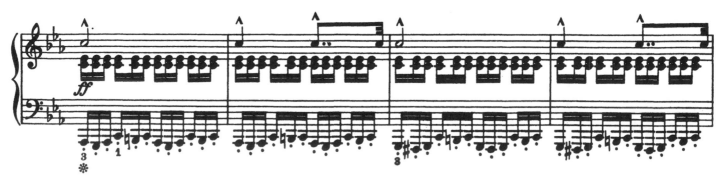

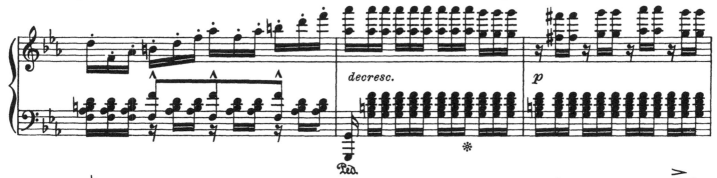

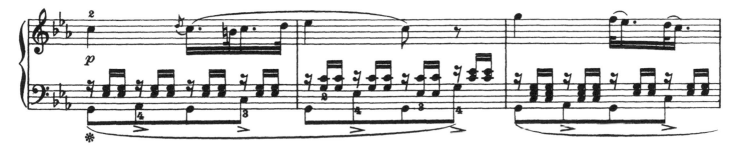

36517

Scherzo.
Allegro vivace.

Trio.

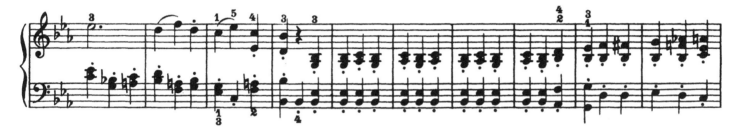

Alla breve.

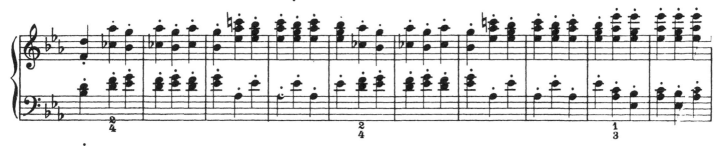

Coda.

Finale.
Allegro molto.

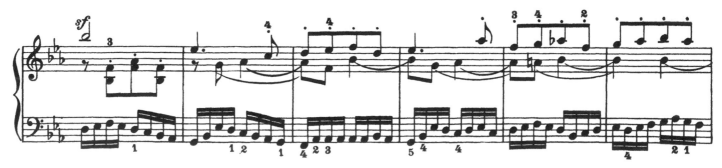

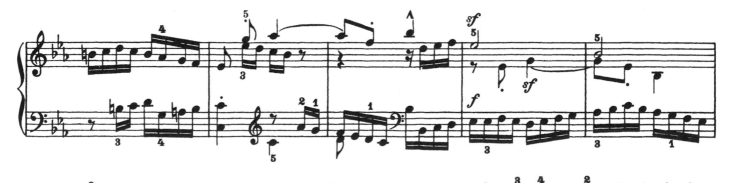

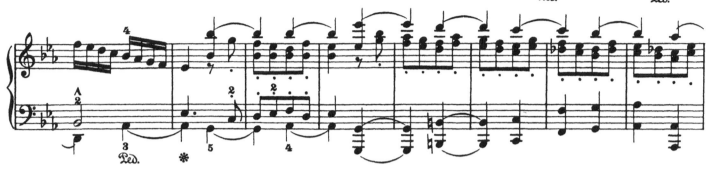

Poco Andante.

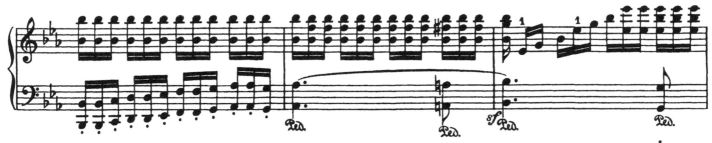

36517

Presto.

SYMPHONY No. 4

Op. 60.

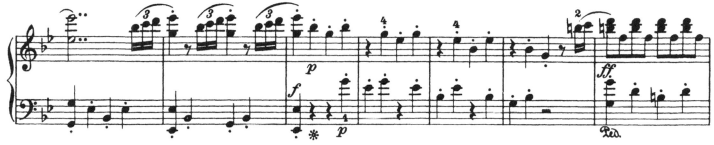

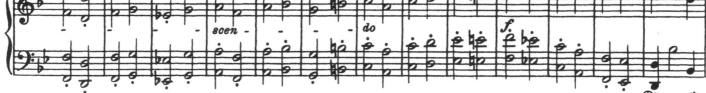

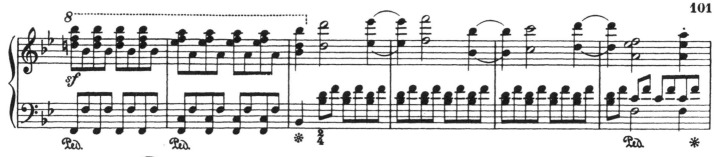

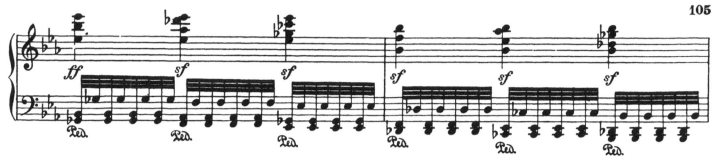

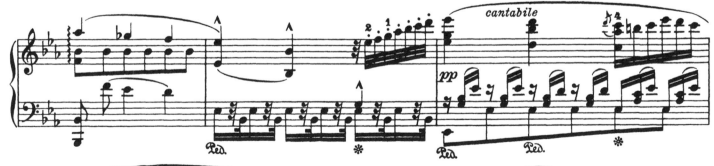

Allegro vivace.

Trio.
Un poco meno mosso.

Un poco meno Allegro.

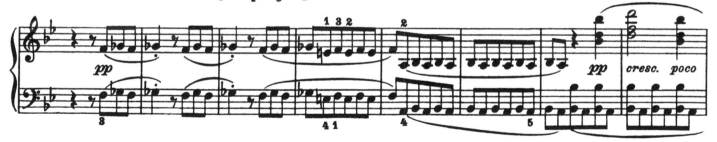

Tempo primo.

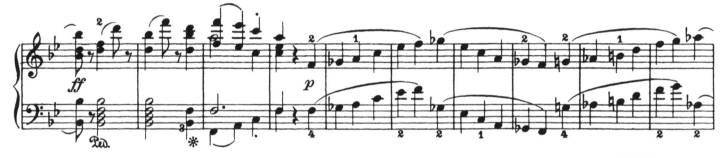

Finale.
Allegro ma non troppo.

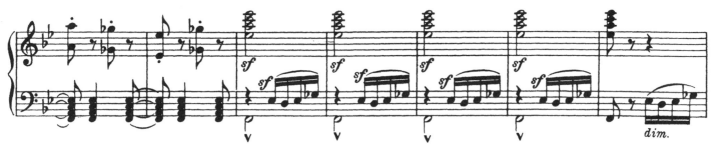

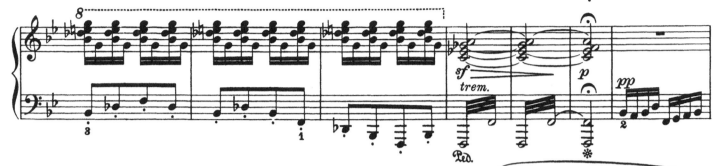

SYMPHONY No. 5

Op. 67.

Allegro con brio.

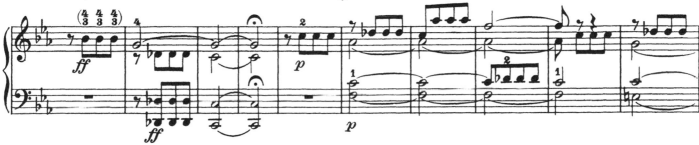

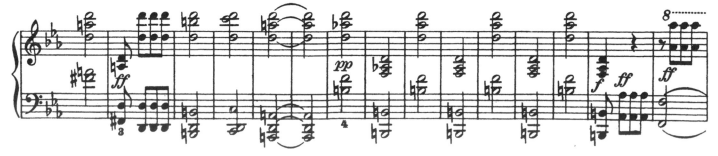

*Andante con moto.

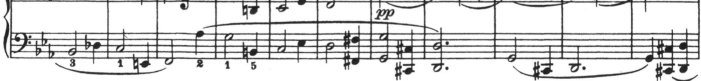

attacca subito

Allegro maestoso.

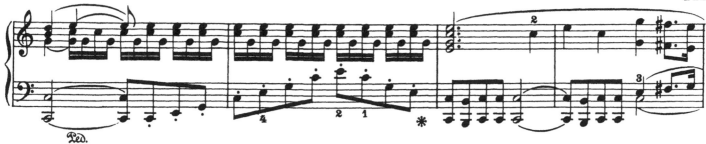

Tempo primo.

Allegro.

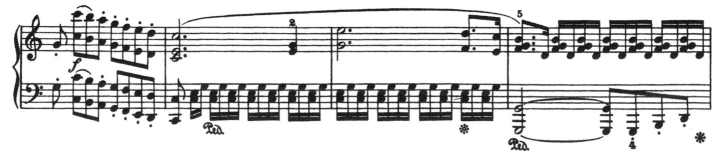

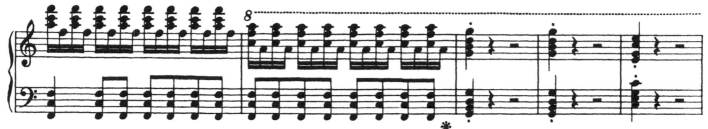